# Praying Problems Out of My Life

*A 13-Week Prayer Devotional Journal*

**International Award-Winning Author
Toneal M. Jackson**

www.WeAreAPS.com

Copyright © 2020 by Toneal M. Jackson

All rights reserved.

No portion of this book may be reproduced mechanically, electronically, or by any other means, including photocopying, without written permission of the publisher.

ISBN: 978-1-945145-59-9

# Author's Note

The purpose of the Prayer Devotional Journal is to lead you into a lifestyle of prayer by becoming more acquainted with God. Prayer is our way of communicating with God. More than just a moment of providing a list of demands (the things we want and need), prayer is a spiritual state of mind. It is a time where we not only speak *to* God but wait to hear *from* God.

Our prayer lives may lack substance because we don't pray on a consistent basis. Oftentimes, I've heard people say, "I don't know how to pray" or even, "I don't know what to pray." This interactive Prayer Devotional Journal is designed to teach methods of prayer. There is a weekly scripture provided, an explanation as to how the given scripture applies to you, as well as a prayer tip that can help improve your prayer life.

# Week 1

## Proverbs 3:5

*"Trust in the Lord with all your heart and lean not to your own understanding."*

## Explanation

You must trust God completely. You must be willing to relinquish control to Him. You must consult with Him regarding every circumstance.

## Prayer Tip

*Ask God to help you relinquish control over your life and grant Him complete control.*

# Monday

How can granting God complete control benefit your partner? Take time to communicate to God why you believe this request to be important for your significant other.

*My prayer for my spouse (partner):*

_____
_____
_____
_____
_____
_____
_____
_____
_____
_____
_____
_____

# Tuesday

How can granting God complete control benefit your child(ren)? Take time to communicate to God why you believe this request to be important for him/her/them.

*My prayer for my child(ren):*

_____
_____
_____
_____
_____
_____
_____
_____
_____
_____
_____
_____
_____
_____

# Wednesday

How can granting God complete control benefit your family? Take time to communicate to God why you believe this request to be important for them.

*My prayer for my family:*

_____
_____
_____
_____
_____
_____
_____
_____
_____
_____
_____
_____
_____

# Thursday

How can granting God complete control benefit your church and pastor? Take time to communicate to God why you believe this request to be important for them.

*My prayer for my church and pastor:*

_____
_____
_____
_____
_____
_____
_____
_____
_____
_____
_____
_____
_____
_____

# Friday

How can granting God complete control benefit your boss/co-workers? Take time to communicate to God why you believe this request to be important for them.

*My prayer for my boss/co-workers:*

_____
_____
_____
_____
_____
_____
_____
_____
_____
_____
_____
_____
_____

# Saturday

How can granting God complete control benefit your enemy? Take time to communicate to God why you believe this request to be important for them.

*My prayer for my enemy/enemies:*

_____
_____
_____
_____
_____
_____
_____
_____
_____
_____
_____
_____
_____
_____

# Sunday

How can granting God complete control benefit you? Take time to communicate to God why you believe this request to be important.

*My prayer for myself:*

_____
_____
_____
_____
_____
_____
_____
_____
_____
_____
_____
_____
_____

# Week 2

## 1 Corinthians 13:7

*"Love never gives up,
never loses faith, is always hopeful,
and endures through every
circumstance."*

## Explanation

Love plays a vital role in our lives.
Not necessarily a reference to
romantic love, but the gift of love
given to us by God.
When executed with the right spirit,
love will always win.

## Prayer Tip

*Pray that God show
you how to love.*

# Monday

How can loving with the love of God benefit your partner? Take time to communicate to God why you believe this request to be important for your significant other.

***My prayer for my spouse (partner):***

_____
_____
_____
_____
_____
_____
_____
_____
_____
_____
_____
_____
_____

# Tuesday

How can loving with the love of God benefit your child(ren)? Take time to communicate to God why you believe this request to be important for him/her/them.

*My prayer for my child(ren):*

_____
_____
_____
_____
_____
_____
_____
_____
_____
_____
_____
_____
_____
_____

# Wednesday

How can loving with the love of God benefit your family? Take time to communicate to God why you believe this request to be important for them.

*My prayer for my family:*

_____
_____
_____
_____
_____
_____
_____
_____
_____
_____
_____
_____

# Thursday

How can loving with the love of God benefit your church and pastor? Take time to communicate to God why you believe this request to be important for them.

*My prayer for my church and pastor:*

_____
_____
_____
_____
_____
_____
_____
_____
_____
_____
_____
_____
_____

# Friday

How can loving with the love of God benefit your boss/co-workers? Take time to communicate to God why you believe this request to be important for them.

*My prayer for my boss/co-workers:*

_____
_____
_____
_____
_____
_____
_____
_____
_____
_____
_____
_____

# Saturday

How can loving with the love of God benefit your enemy? Take time to communicate to God why you believe this request to be important for them.

*My prayer for my enemy/enemies:*

_____
_____
_____
_____
_____
_____
_____
_____
_____
_____
_____
_____
_____

# Sunday

How can loving with the love of God benefit you? Take time to communicate to God why you believe this request to be important.

*My prayer for myself:*

_____
_____
_____
_____
_____
_____
_____
_____
_____
_____
_____
_____

# **Week 3**

## Psalms 139:14

*"I praise you because I am fearfully
and wonderfully made;
your works are wonderful,
I know that full well."*

## Explanation

We should accept that we are
God's workmanship.
Therefore, we should embrace
who we are because
God made us.

## **Prayer Tip**

*Pray that God give you to
love yourself.*

# Monday

How can accepting who we are in God benefit your partner? Take time to communicate to God why you believe this request to be important for your significant other.

*My prayer for my spouse (partner):*

_____
_____
_____
_____
_____
_____
_____
_____
_____
_____
_____

# Tuesday

How can accepting who we are in God benefit your child(ren)? Take time to communicate to God why you believe this request to be important for him/her/them.

*My prayer for my child(ren):*

_____
_____
_____
_____
_____
_____
_____
_____
_____
_____
_____
_____
_____

# Wednesday

How can accepting who we are in God benefit your family? Take time to communicate to God why you believe this request to be important for them.

*My prayer for my family:*

_____
_____
_____
_____
_____
_____
_____
_____
_____
_____
_____
_____
_____

# Thursday

How can accepting who we are in God benefit your church and pastor? Take time to communicate to God why you believe this request to be important for them.

*My prayer for my church and pastor:*

_____
_____
_____
_____
_____
_____
_____
_____
_____
_____
_____
_____
_____

# Friday

How can accepting who we are in God benefit your boss/co-workers? Take time to communicate to God why you believe this request to be important for them.

*My prayer for my boss/co-workers:*

_____
_____
_____
_____
_____
_____
_____
_____
_____
_____
_____
_____
_____

# Saturday

How can accepting who we are in God benefit your enemy? Take time to communicate to God why you believe this request to be important for them.

*My prayer for my enemy/enemies:*

_____
_____
_____
_____
_____
_____
_____
_____
_____
_____
_____
_____
_____
_____
_____

# Sunday

How can accepting who we are in God benefit you? Take time to communicate to God why you believe this request to be important.

*My prayer for myself:*

_____
_____
_____
_____
_____
_____
_____
_____
_____
_____
_____
_____

# **Week 4**

## Joshua 1:9

*"Have I not commanded you?
Be strong and courageous.
Do not be afraid; do not be
discouraged, for the Lord your God
will be with you wherever you go."*

## Explanation

Don't be overcome with fear.
Don't allow your circumstances
to intimidate you.
Take God with you wherever you go,
and you will be victorious.

## **Prayer Tip**

*Pray for courage.*

# Monday

How can possessing courage benefit your partner? Take time to communicate to God why you believe this request to be important for your significant other.

*My prayer for my spouse (partner):*

_____
_____
_____
_____
_____
_____
_____
_____
_____
_____
_____
_____
_____
_____
_____

# Tuesday

How can possessing courage benefit your child(ren)? Take time to communicate to God why you believe this request to be important for him/her/them.

*My prayer for my child(ren):*

_____
_____
_____
_____
_____
_____
_____
_____
_____
_____
_____
_____
_____

# Wednesday

How can possessing courage benefit your family? Take time to communicate to God why you believe this request to be important for them.

*My prayer for my family:*

_____
_____
_____
_____
_____
_____
_____
_____
_____
_____
_____
_____
_____
_____

# Thursday

How can possessing courage benefit your church and pastor? Take time to communicate to God why you believe this request to be important for them.

*My prayer for my church and pastor:*

_____
_____
_____
_____
_____
_____
_____
_____
_____
_____
_____
_____
_____
_____

# Friday

How can possessing courage benefit your boss/co-workers? Take time to communicate to God why you believe this request to be important for them.

*My prayer for my boss/co-workers:*

_____
_____
_____
_____
_____
_____
_____
_____
_____
_____
_____
_____
_____
_____

# Saturday

How can possessing courage benefit your enemy? Take time to communicate to God why you believe this request to be important for them.

*My prayer for my enemy/enemies:*

_____
_____
_____
_____
_____
_____
_____
_____
_____
_____
_____
_____
_____

# Sunday

How can possessing courage benefit you? Take time to communicate to God why you believe this request to be important.

*My prayer for myself:*

_____
_____
_____
_____
_____
_____
_____
_____
_____
_____
_____
_____
_____
_____
_____

# Week 5
## John 14:27

*"Peace I leave with you, my peace I give unto you: not as the world giveth, give I unto you. Let not your heart be troubled, neither let it be afraid."*

## Explanation

Possessing the peace of God is important. Unlike people who may give something and take it back, when God gives you something, you don't have to worry about Him changing His mind.

## Prayer Tip

*Pray for the peace of God.*

# Monday

How can possessing the peace of God benefit your partner? Take time to communicate to God why you believe this request to be important for your significant other.

***My prayer for my spouse (partner):***

_____
_____
_____
_____
_____
_____
_____
_____
_____
_____
_____
_____

# Tuesday

How can possessing the peace of God benefit your child(ren)? Take time to communicate to God why you believe this request to be important for him/her/them.

*My prayer for my child(ren):*

_____
_____
_____
_____
_____
_____
_____
_____
_____
_____
_____
_____
_____
_____

# Wednesday

How can possessing the peace of God benefit your family? Take time to communicate to God why you believe this request to be important for them.

*My prayer for my family:*

_____
_____
_____
_____
_____
_____
_____
_____
_____
_____
_____
_____
_____
_____

# Thursday

How can possessing the peace of God benefit your church and pastor? Take time to communicate to God why you believe this request to be important for them.

**My prayer for my church and pastor:**

_____
_____
_____
_____
_____
_____
_____
_____
_____
_____
_____
_____
_____
_____

# Friday

How can possessing the peace of God benefit your boss/co-workers? Take time to communicate to God why you believe this request to be important for them.

*My prayer for my boss/co-workers:*

_____
_____
_____
_____
_____
_____
_____
_____
_____
_____
_____
_____

# Saturday

How can possessing the peace of God benefit your enemy? Take time to communicate to God why you believe this request to be important for them.

*My prayer for my enemy/enemies:*

_____
_____
_____
_____
_____
_____
_____
_____
_____
_____
_____
_____
_____
_____

# Sunday

How can possessing the peace of God benefit you? Take time to communicate to God why you believe this request to be important.

*My prayer for myself:*

_____
_____
_____
_____
_____
_____
_____
_____
_____
_____
_____
_____

# Week 6

Ephesians 4:32

*"Be kind and compassionate to one another, forgiving each other, just as in Christ God forgave you."*

## Explanation

Always show kindness and compassion to others. Be willing to forgive others because we need God to forgive us.

## Prayer Tip

*Ask God to help you forgive.*

# Monday

How can having a spirit of forgiveness benefit your partner? Take time to communicate to God why you believe this request to be important for your significant other.

*My prayer for my spouse (partner):*

_____
_____
_____
_____
_____
_____
_____
_____
_____
_____
_____
_____

# Tuesday

How can having a spirit of forgiveness benefit your child(ren)? Take time to communicate to God why you believe this request to be important for him/her/them.

*My prayer for my child(ren):*

_____
_____
_____
_____
_____
_____
_____
_____
_____
_____
_____
_____
_____

# Wednesday

How can having a spirit of forgiveness benefit your family? Take time to communicate to God why you believe this request to be important for them.

*My prayer for my family:*

_____
_____
_____
_____
_____
_____
_____
_____
_____
_____
_____
_____
_____
_____

# Thursday

How can having a spirit of forgiveness benefit your church and pastor? Take time to communicate to God why you believe this request to be important for them.

*My prayer for my church and pastor:*

_____
_____
_____
_____
_____
_____
_____
_____
_____
_____
_____
_____
_____
_____

# Friday

How can having a spirit of forgiveness benefit your boss/co-workers? Take time to communicate to God why you believe this request to be important for them.

*My prayer for my boss/co-workers:*

_____
_____
_____
_____
_____
_____
_____
_____
_____
_____
_____
_____
_____

# Saturday

How can having a spirit of forgiveness benefit your enemy? Take time to communicate to God why you believe this request to be important for them.

*My prayer for my enemy/enemies:*

_____
_____
_____
_____
_____
_____
_____
_____
_____
_____
_____
_____
_____
_____
_____

# Sunday

How can having a spirit of forgiveness benefit you? Take time to communicate to God why you believe this request to be important.

*My prayer for myself:*

_____
_____
_____
_____
_____
_____
_____
_____
_____
_____
_____
_____
_____
_____

# Week 7
## 1 Peter 2:9

*"But you are a chosen people, a royal priesthood, a holy nation, God's special possession, that you may declare the praises of him who called you out of darkness into his wonderful light."*

## Explanation

You are handpicked by God.
He chose you to be different.
Stop trying to fit in with everyone because you were purposed to stand out.

## Prayer Tip

*Pray for understanding of who God created you to be.*

# Monday

How can understanding God's purpose benefit your partner? Take time to communicate to God why you believe this request to be important for your significant other.

*My prayer for my spouse (partner):*

_____
_____
_____
_____
_____
_____
_____
_____
_____
_____
_____
_____

# Tuesday

How can understanding God's purpose benefit your child(ren)? Take time to communicate to God why you believe this request to be important for him/her/them.

*My prayer for my child(ren):*

_____
_____
_____
_____
_____
_____
_____
_____
_____
_____
_____
_____
_____
_____
_____

# Wednesday

How can understanding God's purpose benefit your family? Take time to communicate to God why you believe this request to be important for them.

*My prayer for my family:*

_____
_____
_____
_____
_____
_____
_____
_____
_____
_____
_____
_____
_____
_____

# Thursday

How can understanding God's purpose benefit your church and pastor? Take time to communicate to God why you believe this request to be important for them.

***My prayer for my church and pastor:***

_____
_____
_____
_____
_____
_____
_____
_____
_____
_____
_____
_____
_____
_____

# Friday

How can understanding God's purpose benefit your boss/co-workers? Take time to communicate to God why you believe this request to be important for them.

*My prayer for my boss/co-workers:*

_____
_____
_____
_____
_____
_____
_____
_____
_____
_____
_____

# Saturday

How can understanding God's purpose benefit your enemy? Take time to communicate to God why you believe this request to be important for them.

*My prayer for my enemy/enemies:*

_____
_____
_____
_____
_____
_____
_____
_____
_____
_____
_____
_____
_____
_____

# Sunday

How can understanding God's purpose benefit you? Take time to communicate to God why you believe this request to be important.

*My prayer for myself:*

_____
_____
_____
_____
_____
_____
_____
_____
_____
_____
_____
_____
_____
_____

# **Week 8**

## Proverbs 18:10

*"The name of the Lord
is a strong tower;
The righteous run to it
and are safe."*

## Explanation

When you are going through problems, call on the name of the Lord and He will strengthen you. When you are in trouble, He will protect you.

## **Prayer Tip**

*Pray for God's protection.*

# Monday

How can God's protection benefit your partner? Take time to communicate to God why you believe this request to be important for your significant other.

*My prayer for my spouse (partner):*

_____
_____
_____
_____
_____
_____
_____
_____
_____
_____
_____
_____
_____
_____

# Tuesday

How can God's protection benefit your child(ren)? Take time to communicate to God why you believe this request to be important for him/her/them.

*My prayer for my child(ren):*

_____
_____
_____
_____
_____
_____
_____
_____
_____
_____
_____
_____
_____
_____

# Wednesday

How can God's protection benefit your family? Take time to communicate to God why you believe this request to be important for them.

## *My prayer for my family:*

_____
_____
_____
_____
_____
_____
_____
_____
_____
_____
_____
_____
_____

# Thursday

How can God's protection benefit your church and pastor? Take time to communicate to God why you believe this request to be important for them.

***My prayer for my church and pastor:***

_____
_____
_____
_____
_____
_____
_____
_____
_____
_____
_____
_____
_____
_____

# Friday

How can God's protection benefit your boss/co-workers? Take time to communicate to God why you believe this request to be important for them.

*My prayer for my boss/co-workers:*

_____
_____
_____
_____
_____
_____
_____
_____
_____
_____
_____
_____
_____

# Saturday

How can God's protection benefit your enemy? Take time to communicate to God why you believe this request to be important for them.

*My prayer for my enemy/enemies:*

_____
_____
_____
_____
_____
_____
_____
_____
_____
_____
_____
_____
_____

# Sunday

How can God's protection benefit you? Take time to communicate to God why you believe this request to be important.

*My prayer for myself:*

_____
_____
_____
_____
_____
_____
_____
_____
_____
_____
_____
_____
_____

# **Week 9**

Psalms 46:1
*"God is our refuge
and strength,
a very present help
in trouble."*

## Explanation

God doesn't abandon us
when we are going through
difficult situations.
He wants to help us with
our problems.

## **Prayer Tip**

*Ask God to be your strength when
you are overwhelmed.*

# Monday

How can relying on God completely benefit your partner? Take time to communicate to God why you believe this request to be important for your significant other.

*My prayer for my spouse (partner):*

_____
_____
_____
_____
_____
_____
_____
_____
_____
_____
_____
_____

# Tuesday

How can relying on God completely benefit your child(ren)? Take time to communicate to God why you believe this request to be important for him/her/them.

*My prayer for my child(ren):*

_____
_____
_____
_____
_____
_____
_____
_____
_____
_____
_____
_____
_____
_____

# Wednesday

How can relying on God completely benefit your family? Take time to communicate to God why you believe this request to be important for them.

*My prayer for my family:*

_____
_____
_____
_____
_____
_____
_____
_____
_____
_____
_____
_____

# Thursday

How can relying on God completely benefit your church and pastor? Take time to communicate to God why you believe this request to be important for them.

*My prayer for my church and pastor:*

_____
_____
_____
_____
_____
_____
_____
_____
_____
_____
_____
_____
_____
_____

# Friday

How can relying on God completely benefit your boss/co-workers? Take time to communicate to God why you believe this request to be important for them.

*My prayer for my boss/co-workers:*

_____
_____
_____
_____
_____
_____
_____
_____
_____
_____
_____
_____

# Saturday

How can relying on God completely benefit your enemy? Take time to communicate to God why you believe this request to be important for them.

*My prayer for my enemy/enemies:*

_____
_____
_____
_____
_____
_____
_____
_____
_____
_____
_____
_____
_____
_____

# Sunday

How can relying on God completely benefit you? Take time to communicate to God why you believe this request to be important.

*My prayer for myself:*

_____
_____
_____
_____
_____
_____
_____
_____
_____
_____
_____
_____

# **Week 10**
## 1 Peter 4:8

*"Most important of all,
continue to show deep love
for each other, for love covers a
multitude of sins."*

## Explanation

You must always
be able to demonstrate
the love of God to others
despite the situation.

## **Prayer Tip**

*Ask God to show you how to love
unconditionally.*

# Monday

How can displaying unconditional love benefit your partner? Take time to communicate to God why you believe this request to be important for your significant other.

*My prayer for my spouse (partner):*

_____
_____
_____
_____
_____
_____
_____
_____
_____
_____
_____

# Tuesday

How can displaying unconditional love benefit your child(ren)? Take time to communicate to God why you believe this request to be important for him/her/them.

*My prayer for my child(ren):*

_____
_____
_____
_____
_____
_____
_____
_____
_____
_____
_____
_____
_____
_____

# Wednesday

How can displaying unconditional love benefit your family? Take time to communicate to God why you believe this request to be important for them.

*My prayer for my family:*

_____
_____
_____
_____
_____
_____
_____
_____
_____
_____
_____
_____

# Thursday

How can displaying unconditional love benefit your church and pastor? Take time to communicate to God why you believe this request to be important for them.

***My prayer for my church and pastor:***

_____
_____
_____
_____
_____
_____
_____
_____
_____
_____
_____
_____
_____

# Friday

How can displaying unconditional love benefit your boss/co-workers? Take time to communicate to God why you believe this request to be important for them.

*My prayer for my boss/co-workers:*

_____
_____
_____
_____
_____
_____
_____
_____
_____
_____
_____
_____
_____
_____

# Saturday

How can displaying unconditional love benefit your enemy? Take time to communicate to God why you believe this request to be important for them.

*My prayer for my enemy/enemies:*

_____
_____
_____
_____
_____
_____
_____
_____
_____
_____
_____
_____
_____

# Sunday

How can displaying unconditional love benefit you? Take time to communicate to God why you believe this request to be important.

*My prayer for myself:*

_____
_____
_____
_____
_____
_____
_____
_____
_____
_____
_____
_____
_____

# **Week 11**

## Luke 12:7

*"And the very hairs on your head are all numbered. So don't be afraid; you are more valuable to God than a whole flock of sparrows."*

## Explanation

God knows everything about you – including the number of hairs on your head. So, if He takes the time to know about the "small" things, that shows how valuable you are.

## **Prayer Tip**

*Ask God to show you how to value yourself.*

# Monday

How can understanding self-worth benefit your partner? Take time to communicate to God why you believe this request to be important for your significant other.

*My prayer for my spouse (partner):*

_____
_____
_____
_____
_____
_____
_____
_____
_____
_____
_____
_____
_____
_____

# Tuesday

How can understanding self-worth benefit your child(ren)? Take time to communicate to God why you believe this request to be important for him/her/them.

*My prayer for my child(ren):*

_____
_____
_____
_____
_____
_____
_____
_____
_____
_____
_____
_____
_____
_____

# Wednesday

How can understanding self-worth benefit your family? Take time to communicate to God why you believe this request to be important for them.

*My prayer for my family:*

_____
_____
_____
_____
_____
_____
_____
_____
_____
_____
_____
_____
_____
_____

# Thursday

How can understanding self-worth benefit your church and pastor? Take time to communicate to God why you believe this request to be important for them.

*My prayer for my church and pastor:*

_____
_____
_____
_____
_____
_____
_____
_____
_____
_____
_____
_____
_____
_____
_____

# Friday

How can understanding self-worth benefit your boss/co-workers? Take time to communicate to God why you believe this request to be important for them.

*My prayer for my boss/co-workers:*

# Saturday

How can understanding self-worth benefit your enemy? Take time to communicate to God why you believe this request to be important for them.

*My prayer for my enemy/enemies:*

# Sunday

How can understanding self-worth benefit you? Take time to communicate to God why you believe this request to be important.

*My prayer for myself:*

_____
_____
_____
_____
_____
_____
_____
_____
_____
_____
_____
_____
_____

# Week 12

## Isaiah 41:10

*"So do not fear, for I am with you; do not be dismayed, for I am your God. I will strengthen you and help you; I will uphold you with my righteous right hand."*

## Explanation

We have no need to be fearful of anything because God is with us. He will always be with us and help however necessary.

## Prayer Tip

*Pray that the spirit of pride does not overtake you.*

# Monday

How can overcoming the spirit of pride benefit your partner? Take time to communicate to God why you believe this request to be important for your significant other.

***My prayer for my spouse (partner):***

_____
_____
_____
_____
_____
_____
_____
_____
_____
_____
_____
_____

# Tuesday

How can overcoming the spirit of pride benefit your child(ren)? Take time to communicate to God why you believe this request to be important for him/her/them.

*My prayer for my child(ren):*

___
___
___
___
___
___
___
___
___
___
___
___
___

# Wednesday

How can overcoming the spirit of pride benefit your family? Take time to communicate to God why you believe this request to be important for them.

*My prayer for my family:*

_____
_____
_____
_____
_____
_____
_____
_____
_____
_____
_____
_____
_____

# Thursday

How can overcoming the spirit of pride benefit your church and pastor? Take time to communicate to God why you believe this request to be important for them.

*My prayer for my church and pastor:*

_____
_____
_____
_____
_____
_____
_____
_____
_____
_____
_____
_____
_____
_____

# Friday

How can overcoming the spirit of pride benefit your boss/co-workers? Take time to communicate to God why you believe this request to be important for them.

*My prayer for my boss/co-workers:*

_____
_____
_____
_____
_____
_____
_____
_____
_____
_____
_____
_____
_____
_____

# Saturday

How can overcoming the spirit of pride benefit your enemy? Take time to communicate to God why you believe this request to be important for them.

*My prayer for my enemy/enemies:*

_____
_____
_____
_____
_____
_____
_____
_____
_____
_____
_____
_____
_____
_____

# Sunday

How can overcoming the spirit of pride benefit you? Take time to communicate to God why you believe this request to be important.

*My prayer for myself:*

_____
_____
_____
_____
_____
_____
_____
_____
_____
_____
_____
_____

# **Week 13**

## Psalms 55:22

*"Give your burdens to the Lord,
and He will take care of you.
He will not permit the godly
to slip and fall."*

## Explanation

Whatever is bothering you or
causing you to worry, give it to God.
When you belong to Him,
He won't allow bad things to
overtake you.

## **Prayer Tip**

*Pray that God removes worry
and replaces it with faith.*

# Monday

How can operating in faith benefit your partner? Take time to communicate to God why you believe this request to be important for your significant other.

*My prayer for my spouse (partner):*

_____
_____
_____
_____
_____
_____
_____
_____
_____
_____
_____
_____
_____
_____

# Tuesday

How can operating in faith benefit your child(ren)? Take time to communicate to God why you believe this request to be important for him/her/them.

*My prayer for my child(ren):*

_____
_____
_____
_____
_____
_____
_____
_____
_____
_____
_____
_____
_____

# Wednesday

How can operating in faith benefit your family? Take time to communicate to God why you believe this request to be important for them.

*My prayer for my family:*

_____
_____
_____
_____
_____
_____
_____
_____
_____
_____
_____
_____
_____

# Thursday

How can operating in faith benefit your church and pastor? Take time to communicate to God why you believe this request to be important for them.

***My prayer for my church and pastor:***

_____
_____
_____
_____
_____
_____
_____
_____
_____
_____
_____
_____
_____
_____
_____

# Friday

How can operating in faith benefit your boss/co-workers? Take time to communicate to God why you believe this request to be important for them.

*My prayer for my boss/co-workers:*

_____
_____
_____
_____
_____
_____
_____
_____
_____
_____
_____
_____
_____

# Saturday

How can operating in faith benefit your enemy? Take time to communicate to God why you believe this request to be important for them.

*My prayer for my enemy/enemies:*

_____
_____
_____
_____
_____
_____
_____
_____
_____
_____
_____
_____
_____
_____

# Sunday

How can operating in faith benefit you? Take time to communicate to God why you believe this request to be important.

*My prayer for myself:*

_____
_____
_____
_____
_____
_____
_____
_____
_____
_____
_____
_____
_____
_____

# Epilogue

The hope is that now that you have reached the end of this journal, you have learned:

- Prayer is not just about you
- How to pray more effectively
- How to cope with your problems

I also pray that you have less problems than you had 13 weeks ago. My desire is that you have a true understanding of the source of your problems. Despite whatever problems you encounter, remember to continually trust God.

Toneal M. Jackson is a National and International Award-Winning Author; Publisher; and Inspirational Speaker. She is the founder of Artists Promoting Success, as well as #ImGladToBeAWoman, an organization that empowers women.

In 2012, CBS Chicago named her one of "5 Indie Authors and Publishers to Watch Out For". She was inducted into the Young Women's Professional League in 2016 and POWER (Professional Organization of Women of Excellence Recognized) in 2018. In 2019, she received the I Change Nations Award for her work in the literary industry. For more on Toneal, visit: www.AWEInspiringCoach.com

## **Other Books by Toneal M. Jackson:**

*Pleasing Your Partner: A Spiritual Guide to H.A.P.P.I.N.E.S.S.*
*Four Girls: A Lot of Choices*
*Four Girls Learn Their Colors*
*It's A Way to Say It All: How to Communicate with Your Kids*
*It's A Way to Say It All: How to Communicate with Your Partner*
*Growing Up to be Happy*
*She's Out. I'm In*
*Inspiration from A.B.O.V.E.*
*Learning to Love Me*
*Love Me...Please*
*Being an Authorpreneur: How to Succeed in the Book Business*
*The Race to the Ring: The Seven Cs of a Successful Courtship*
*The Fruit of the Spirit Anthology:*
*Taking Life's Bitter Moments and Making Them Sweet*
*Praying Peace Over My Life (Journal)*
*Praying Purpose for My Life (Journal)*
*Praying Prosperity into My Life (Journal)*
*Praising through the Pandemic*

www.ingramcontent.com/pod-product-compliance
Lightning Source LLC
LaVergne TN
LVHW020936090426
835512LV00020B/3382